Sign Language

My First 100 Words

Illustrated by Michiyo Nelson

Cartwheel BOOKS®

SCHOLASTIC INC.

New York Toronto London Auckland Sydney
Mexico City New Delhi Hong Kong Buenos Aires

For my two precious boys, Luke and Sam
—M.N.

Library of Congress Cataloging-in-Publication Data

Nelson, Michiyo.
Sign language : my first 100 words / illustrated by Michiyo Nelson.
p. cm.
Includes index.
ISBN-10: 0-545-05657-8   ISBN-13: 978-0-545-05657-1
1. American Sign Language--Juvenile literature.
2. Deaf--Means of communication--United States--Juvenile literature. I. Title.
HV2476.S53 2008   419'.7--dc22   2008006906

ISBN-13: 978-0-545-05657-1
ISBN-10: 0-545-05657-8

10 9 8 7 6 5 4 3 2   8 9 10 11 12

Printed in the U.S.A.
First printing, June 2008

Design by Theresa Venezia
Edited by Erika Lo and Jacqueline Bernacki

Table of Contents

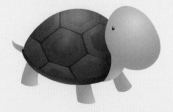

Introduction

American Sign Language (ASL) is the most common type of sign language used in the United States. ASL allows people who are deaf or hearing impaired to "talk" with each other and hearing people. Many people—both deaf and hearing—use ASL. Some people learn ASL to communicate with family members or friends; others choose to learn ASL as a second language.

ASL is a real language, like English or Spanish, because ASL has its own grammatical rules, word order, and slang expressions. Signs can change slightly in different parts of the country, in the same way that spoken English has different accents. This book uses signs that are commonly used throughout the United States.

ASL uses many different types of signs. Signs can be one-handed, two-handed, one step, or more than one step. They can be held in one position or include movement. This book will show you how to make different types of signs and teach you 100 simple signs for everyday use.

Your Signing Space

Your signing space usually reaches from the top of your head to your waist and from shoulder to shoulder. Imagine a box around this area. Keep your signs in this space so that other people can see your hands clearly.

Using Your Hands

To sign the words in this book, follow the handshapes shown. You should imagine yourself in the position of the children who are pictured. Your hands should face the person you are signing to, just as the illustrated signs face you. Look at the placement of the hands in the illustration. If they are closer to the shoulders or nose, your hands should be in the same location near your own body.

Signs can change depending on whether the signer is right-handed or left-handed. (In this book some of the children signing are right-handed, and some are left-handed.) For one-handed signs, you can use the hand you write with. For two-handed signs, you can use your writing hand as the signing hand with more movement.

In this book some of the signs that use movement will include an arrow. Move your hands in the direction shown by the arrow, and follow the shape of the arrow. If the arrow is straight and points down, your hand should move downward in a straight line.

Faces and Expressions

Faces and expressions are important in ASL. Some signs should be combined with the feelings they represent. You will see that the Feelings signs in this book are shown with both signing hands and a matching facial expression. If you are signing the word for *angry*, your face should look angry. Your hand can also move in a quick, angry movement, as if you were really mad!

Spelling Out Words

Each letter of the English alphabet has its own hand-shape in ASL. You can use the signed alphabet to fingerspell words. Fingerspelling is an important part of learning ASL. It is used for the names of people and places and can also be used for words without a specific sign. Practice fingerspelling your name, so you can introduce yourself to others. And if there is a word you don't know the sign for, try spelling it out!

Some signs use letters from the ASL alphabet. The sign for *television* is the letters **T** and **V**. The sign for the color *green* uses the letter **G**. When a sign uses a signed letter in this book, the letter will be put in bold type in the explanation beside the illustration.

Be Creative

Keep in mind that signs can be combined to form new words. For example, the signs for *food* and *store* can be signed together to indicate a grocery store or supermarket. The sign for *teacher* combines the signs for *teach* (step 1) and *person/doer* (step 2). You could also combine the signs for *dance* and *person/doer* to form the word *dancer*!

Negatives

You can make a sentence or expression negative by shaking your head or making negative expressions while signing. For example, if you shake your head and sign the word *sleepy*, that would mean you are not sleepy.

Memorizing the Signs

As you study the ASL signs in this book, you will notice that some signs imitate the objects they represent. In the sign for *bird*, fingers open and close by the mouth like a beak. The sign for *rainbow* curves, just like a real rainbow. You can use these clues to help you remember new signs!

Let's Start Signing!

Now that you know how to read the signs in this book, you can use it to learn new signs or practice the ones you already know. ASL may seem hard at first, but the best way to learn any new language is to practice with another person! You can practice with someone who already knows ASL, or you can find a friend or family member who wants to learn ASL, too. The more you use sign language, the easier it will become!

grandfather

Bounce your hand away from your forehead.

grandmother

Bounce your hand away from your chin.

brother

Touch your forehead. Bring your wrists together.

sister

Draw your thumb down along your jaw. Bring your wrists together.

grandfather

grandmother

brother

sister

Family

cousin

dad

cousin

dad

mom

baby

cousin

Wiggle the letter **C**.

dad

Touch your thumb to your forehead.

mom

Touch your thumb to your chin.

baby

Swing your arms in a rocking motion.

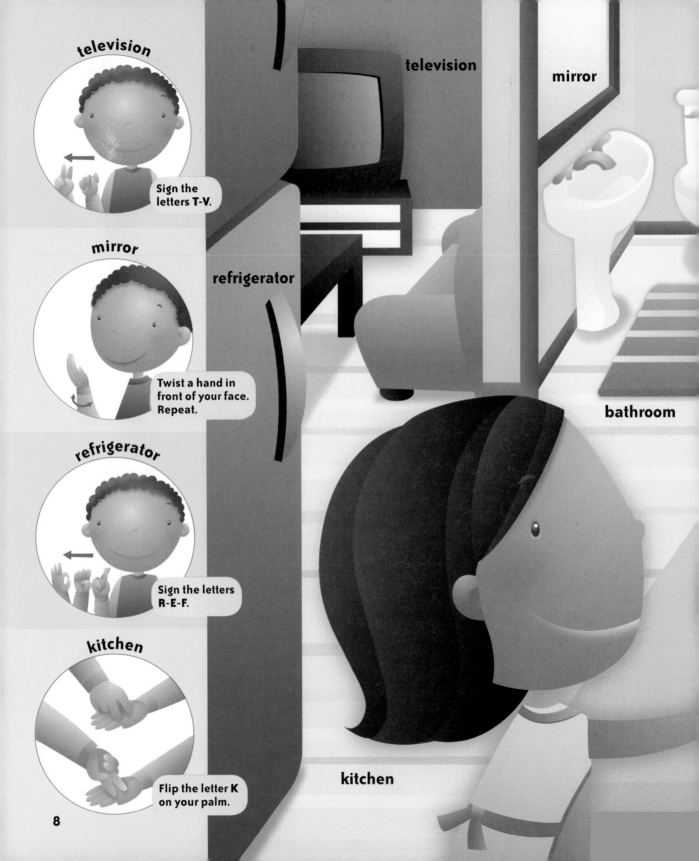

television

Sign the letters **T-V.**

mirror

Twist a hand in front of your face. Repeat.

refrigerator

Sign the letters **R-E-F.**

kitchen

Flip the letter **K** on your palm.

television

mirror

refrigerator

bathroom

kitchen

8

Home

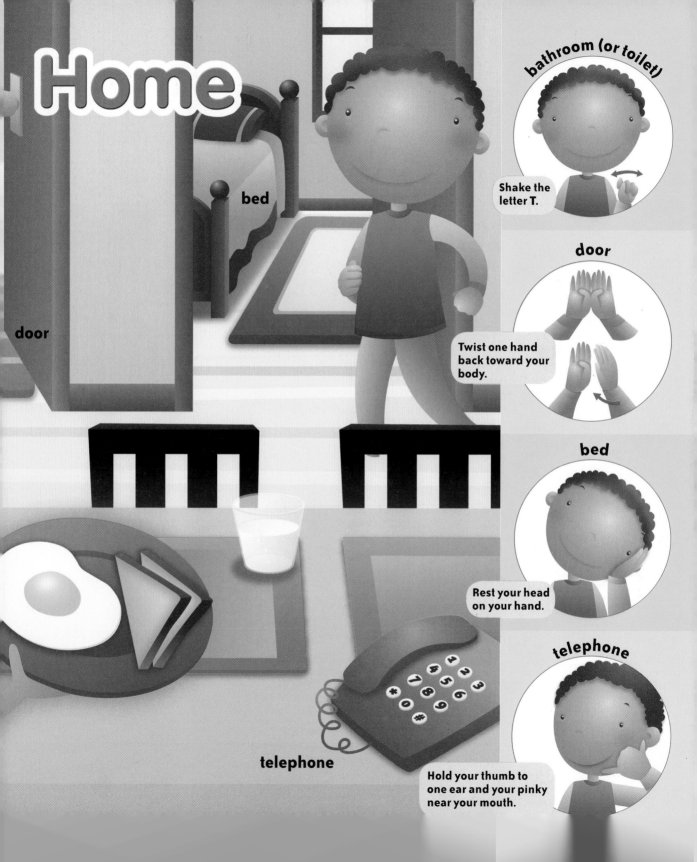

door

bed

telephone

bathroom (or toilet)

Shake the letter T.

door

Twist one hand back toward your body.

bed

Rest your head on your hand.

telephone

Hold your thumb to one ear and your pinky near your mouth.

Food

eat (or food)

Touch your mouth twice.

water

Tap the letter W against your chin. Repeat.

sandwich

Hold one hand and pull it toward your mouth.

orange

Squeeze a fist in front of your mouth. Repeat.

water

sandwich

orange

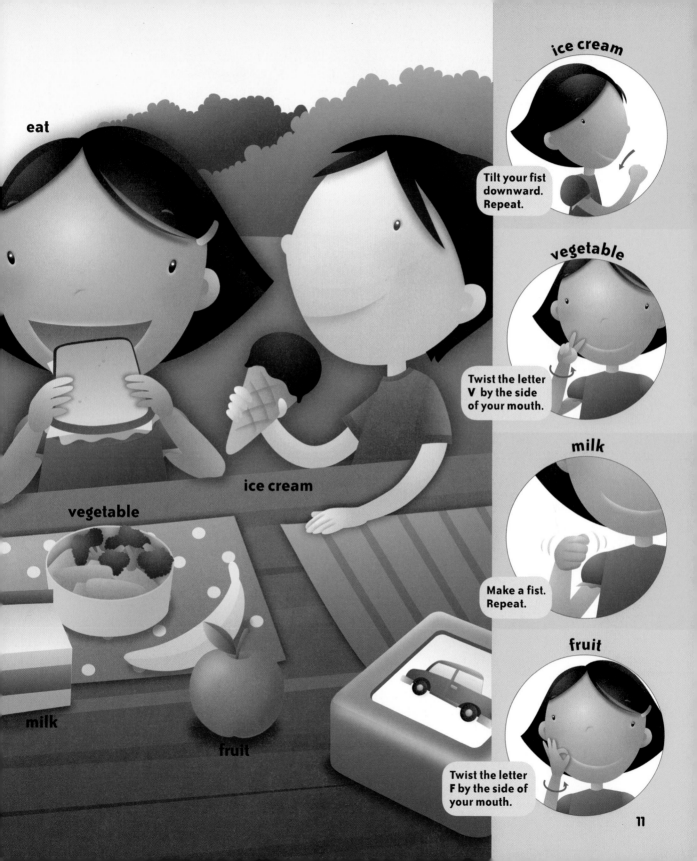

black

Draw your finger across your forehead.

white

Move your hand away from you while bringing your fingers together.

red

Touch your lips and draw your finger downward.

blue

Wiggle the letter **B**.

rainbow

white

purple

black

yellow

red

blue

12

Colors

green

yellow

Wiggle the letter **Y**.

green

Wiggle the letter **G**.

purple

Wiggle the letter **P**.

rainbow

Touch 4 fingers from each hand together. Draw a curve through the air.

* See page 10 for *orange*.   **13**

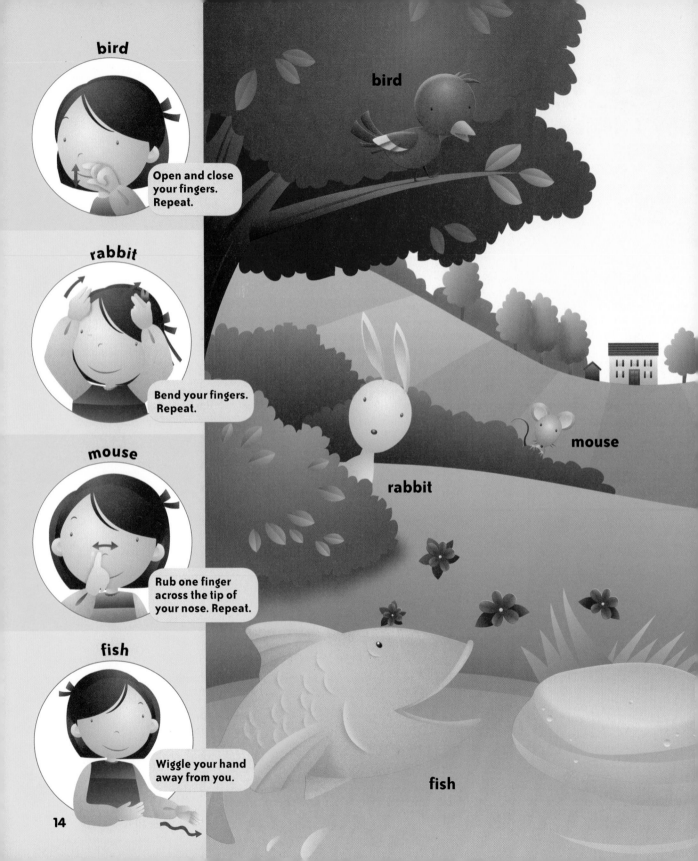

bird

Open and close your fingers. Repeat.

rabbit

Bend your fingers. Repeat.

mouse

Rub one finger across the tip of your nose. Repeat.

fish

Wiggle your hand away from you.

bird

rabbit

mouse

fish

14

Animals

dog

cat

turtle

bug

dog
1. Pat your leg.
2. Snap your fingers twice.

cat
Pinch your fingers & pull them away from your cheeks. Repeat.

turtle
Stick out and wiggle your covered thumb.

bug
Bend the two upright fingers. Repeat.

Neighborhood

hospital

Draw a cross on your arm with the letter **H**.

library

Move the letter **L** in a circle. Repeat.

store (or market)

Swing your hands away from the middle of your chest. Repeat.

car

Move your hands up and down in a curve. Repeat.

hospital

LIBRARY

TOWN MARKET

store

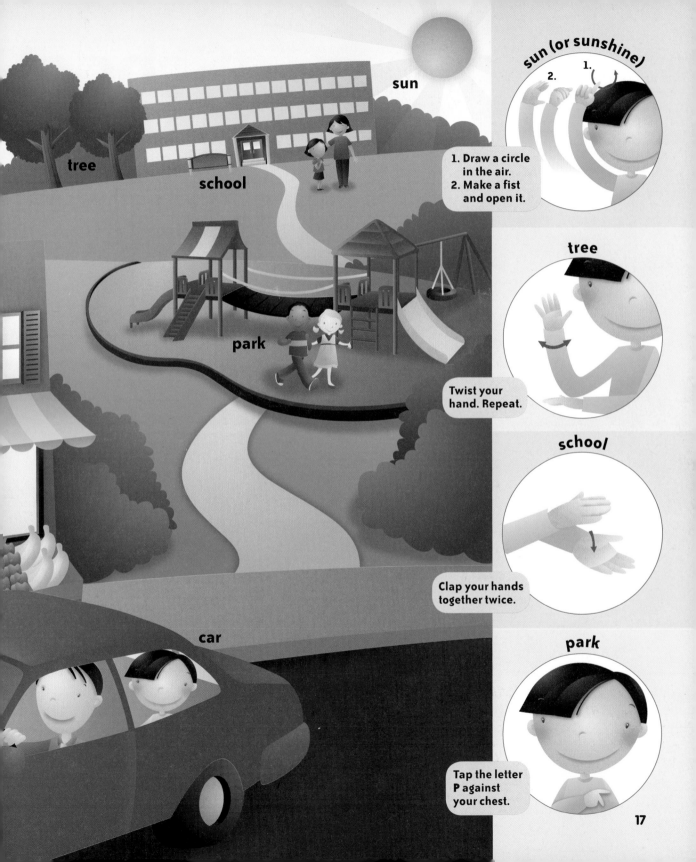

sun

tree

school

park

car

sun (or sunshine)
1.
2.

1. Draw a circle
in the air.
2. Make a fist
and open it.

tree

Twist your
hand. Repeat.

school

Clap your hands
together twice.

park

Tap the letter
P against
your chest.

17

School

paper

Brush your top palm against your bottom palm. Repeat.

book

Open your touching palms.

teacher

1.
2.

1. Move your hands away from your head.
2. Move them down the sides of your body.

scissors

Open and close your fingers while moving them to the side.

paper

book

teacher

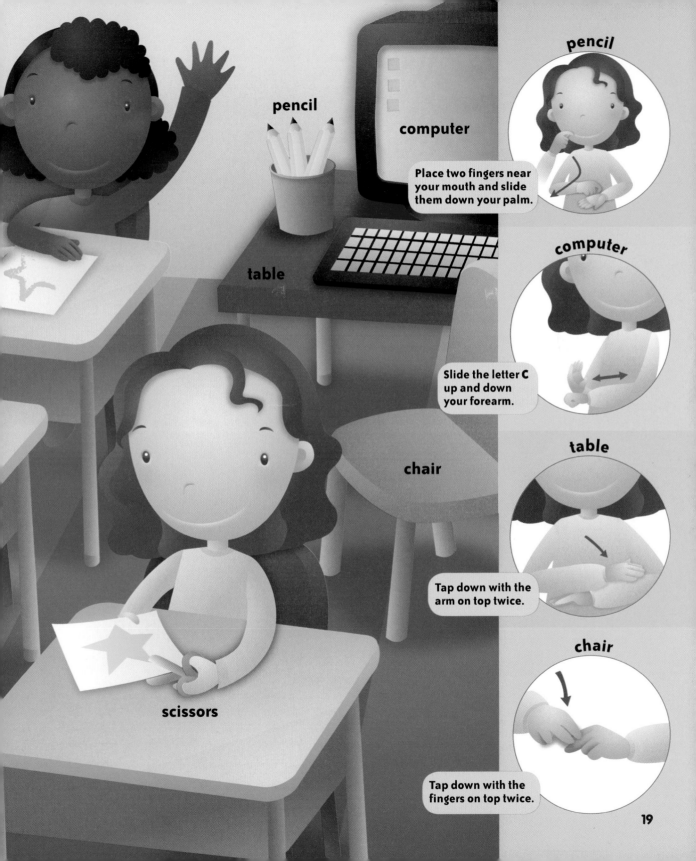

pencil

computer

pencil

Place two fingers near your mouth and slide them down your palm.

table

computer

Slide the letter **C** up and down your forearm.

chair

table

Tap down with the arm on top twice.

scissors

chair

Tap down with the fingers on top twice.

19

race

Move your hands back and forth alternately.

dance

Swing two fingers over your other hand. Repeat.

basketball

Flick your wrists forward twice.

swim

Move your hands out and away from each other. Repeat.

race

dance

SPORT CENTE

basketball   swim

20

Sports

bicycle

bicycle

Pedal both fists forward.

baseball (or softball)

Tilt both fists forward. Repeat.

soccer

Tap the bottom hand against your top hand twice.

football

Lace your fingers together. Repeat.

baseball   soccer   football

21

girl

Draw your thumb down your jaw.

boy

Touch your top fingers to your thumb. Repeat.

you

Point your finger away from your chest.

I (or me)

Touch your finger to your chest.

girl

boy

doctor

you

me

People

friend

firefighter

police officer

friend

1.

2.

1. Link your index fingers.
2. Repeat with a different hand on top.

doctor

Touch the letter **D** to your wrist.

firefighter

Fold in your thumb and touch your hand to your forehead.

police officer (or cop)

Place the letter **C** over the left side of your chest.

23

excited

Bend your middle fingers. Pedal your hands away from your chest.

angry

Bend your fingers and pull them away from your face.

bored

Twist your finger forward against the side of your nose.

sleepy

Flap your fingers in front of your eyes.

angry

excited

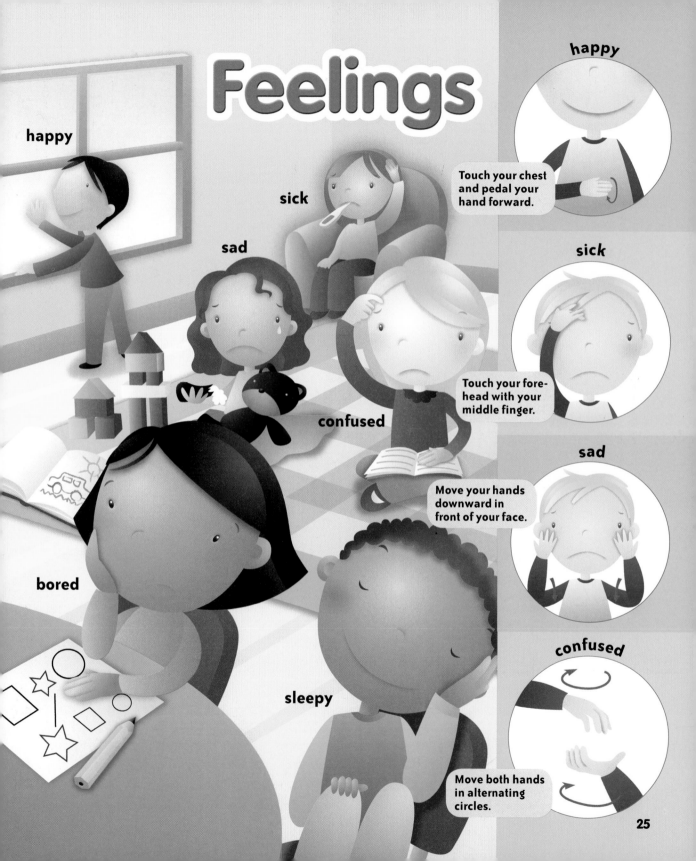

Feelings

happy

sick

sad

confused

bored

sleepy

happy

Touch your chest and pedal your hand forward.

sick

Touch your forehead with your middle finger.

sad

Move your hands downward in front of your face.

confused

Move both hands in alternating circles.

25

sign (or sign language)

Pedal your hands toward your chest.

I love you

Combine the letters **I**, **L**, and **Y**.

excuse me

Brush your fingertips over your palm. Repeat.

sorry

Make a circle over your heart with your fist.

Excuse me!

I love you!

Conversation

Sorry!

Thank you.

Please.

My name is...

Hello!

thank you
Swing a hand down from your mouth with your palm facing up.

please
Make a circle over your heart.

name (or My name is...)
Tap down with the fingers on top twice.

hello
Touch your forehead and wave your hand.

Numbers

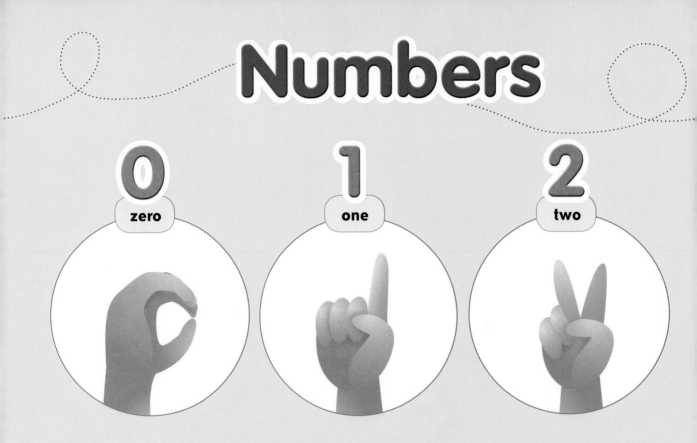

0 zero
1 one
2 two

6 six
7 seven
8 eight

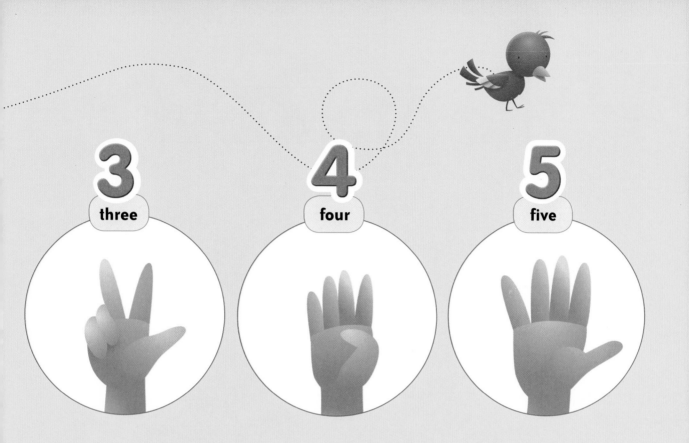

3 three

4 four

5 five

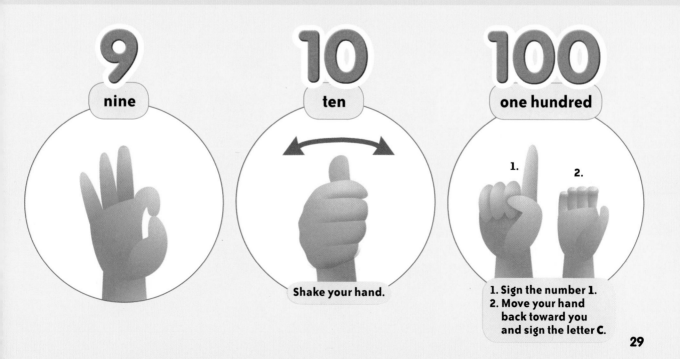

9 nine

10 ten

Shake your hand.

100 one hundred

1.

2.

1. Sign the number 1.
2. Move your hand back toward you and sign the letter C.

The Alphabet

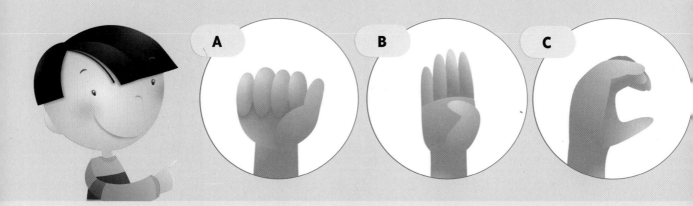

A B C

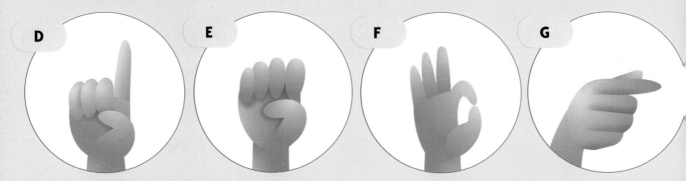

D E F G

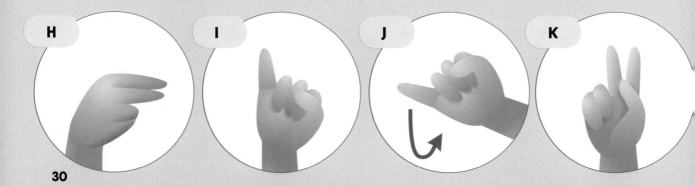

H I J K

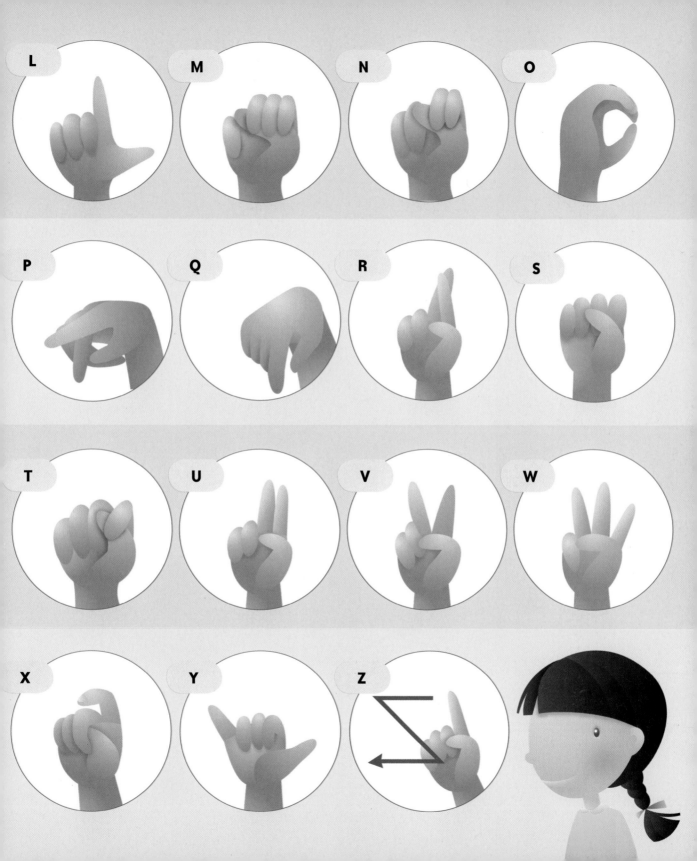

Index